# BEYOND THE LAUNCH

Essential Lessons

From

Growing A Startup

*Marion Parker*

Copyright © 2024 by Marion Parker

All Rights Reserved.

Executive Editor: Rachel Zhang

First Edition: August 2024.

No parts of this publication may be reproduced, distributed, or transmitted in any form or by any means, including photocopying, recording, or other electronic or mechanical methods, or by any information storage and retrieval system without the prior written permission of the author.

The information contained within this book is strictly for educational purposes. If you wish to apply ideas contained in this book, you are taking full responsibility for your actions.

"Never confuse a single defeat with a final defeat."
— F. Scott Fitzgerald

**TABLE OF CONTENTS**

Introduction _____ 6
   1. The Journey Begins _____ 6
Part I: Laying the Foundation _____ 9
   2. Defining Your Vision and Mission _____ 9
   3. Building the Right Team _____ 13
   4. Creating a Positive Work Environment _____ 16
   5. Mastering Communication and Decision-Making _____ 19
Part II: Managing Growth and Challenges _____ 24
   6. Avoiding Common Pitfalls _____ 24
   7. Financial Management and Resource Allocation _____ 27
   8. Strategic Planning and Execution _____ 30
   9. Building a Strong Sales Strategy _____ 36
Part III: Navigating the Entrepreneurial Journey _____ 42
   10. Learning from Failures and Mistakes _____ 42
   11. Legal and Compliance Issues _____ 46
   12. Customer Relationship Management _____ 52
   13. Delegation and Leadership _____ 56
   14. Maintaining Personal Well-Being _____ 61
Part IV: Future-Proofing Your Startup _____ 66
   15. Scaling and Sustaining Growth _____ 66
   16. Adapting to Market Changes _____ 71
   17. Sustainable Business Practices _____ 75
   18. Innovation and Improvement _____ 79
One Last Thing... _____ 84

# Introduction

## 1. The Journey Begins

> In this chapter you will find
>
> 1. Why I Wrote This Book
> 2. What You'll Learn

Creating and building a business is challenging, painful, and, at times, disheartening. The odds of achieving something truly rewarding or profitable are slim. I'm not here to scare you—it's just the reality of the statistics. Frankly, I try to avoid looking at them too often because they can be overwhelmingly discouraging. Take a moment to examine the statistics in your country… and if you still feel brave, keep reading this book.

Today, I'm writing from Spain. I've been here for a couple of weeks visiting an old friend. During our conversations, she mentioned that here, 51% of new businesses close within the first four years. And startups? When I asked, she informed me that 9 out of 10 startups fail within the first three years. Why is this the case? According to *CB Insights*, a global consultancy firm, the most common reasons include not addressing a real problem, running out of cash, having the wrong team, failing to analyze competitors, setting incorrect prices, having an unclear business model, and a lack of focus, among other factors.

This book is not about theory, concepts, or information you can easily find on the web. Instead, I want to share my personal views and experiences from three consecutive failures followed by one final success. If I could go back in time, I would have loved for someone to warn me about the pitfalls and challenges ahead. I hope that by sharing my journey, I can provide insights that will resonate with you and help you navigate your own path.

## Why I Wrote This Book

The entrepreneurial journey is filled with highs and lows, moments of doubt, and occasional triumphs. My journey has been no different. I've experienced the euphoria of launching a new venture and the crushing disappointment of seeing it fail. Yet, each failure taught me invaluable lessons that ultimately led to my success.

I wrote this book to offer a candid, unfiltered look at what it takes to grow a startup. While countless resources provide theoretical knowledge, few delve into the gritty, real-world experiences that shape an entrepreneur's path. My goal is to bridge that gap by sharing my story, including the mistakes I've made and the lessons I've learned along the way.

I want to demystify the process of building a business and provide practical insights that you can apply to your journey. This book is for those who are passionate about their ideas and determined to turn them into successful ventures, despite the odds. It's for anyone who has ever faced setbacks and wondered if they should keep going.

## What You'll Learn

In this book, I want to take you through the real-life challenges and triumphs of growing a startup, based on my personal experiences. We'll dive into how to hire the right people—not just those with impressive resumes, but those who genuinely fit your company culture and understand your business. Building a team that works well together is crucial, and I'll share tips on creating a positive work environment where everyone feels valued and motivated.

Communication is key in any business. I'll talk about how to make sure your team is on the same page and how to encourage open and honest discussions. We'll also cover decision-making—when to listen, when to lead, and how to avoid being the bottleneck that slows everything down.

I'll be honest about the common pitfalls that many startups face, like running out of money or losing focus. These are hard lessons I've learned the hard way, and I want to help you avoid them. Managing your finances and resources wisely is another big topic. I'll share practical advice on keeping your cash flow healthy and making smart financial decisions.

Strategic planning is another critical area. Together, we'll explore how to create effective strategies and, more importantly, how to execute them. I'll also delve into building a solid sales strategy—understanding the importance of having a reliable sales team and setting realistic forecasts.

Failure is a part of the journey, and I'll show you how to embrace and learn from it. I'll share stories from my own setbacks and how they ultimately led to success. Leadership and delegation are also vital skills. I'll offer insights on how to delegate effectively and lead without micromanaging.

Taking care of yourself is just as important as taking care of your business. We'll talk about maintaining a work-life balance, staying healthy, and finding time for your personal life. Lastly, I'll provide strategies for future-proofing your startup—how to scale, adapt to changes, and keep growing sustainably.

Each chapter is filled with practical advice, personal anecdotes, and actionable insights. My hope is that this book will serve as a guide and a source of inspiration as you navigate the complexities of growing your own startup. The road ahead is tough, but with the right knowledge and mindset, you can increase your chances of success.

So, let's begin this journey together. Beyond the launch, there's a world of opportunities and challenges waiting to be explored.

# Part I: Laying the Foundation

## 2. Defining Your Vision and Mission

In this chapter you will find:

- Crafting a Compelling Vision Statement
- Aligning Your Mission with Business Goals
- Communicating Your Vision to the Team

I know.. this is something we have to do even though (unfortunately) some execs don't see much value in this. Keep in mind that a clear and compelling vision and mission are the foundation of any successful startup. They serve as a guiding light, providing direction and purpose for your business. In this chapter, we'll take a look at how to craft a vision statement, align your mission with business goals, and effectively communicate your vision to your people.

**Crafting a Compelling Vision Statement**

Your vision statement is <u>a snapshot of your future aspirations</u>.

*Example: Google's vision statement.*

*To provide access to the world's information in one click.*

A vision statement should inspire and motivate, providing a picture of what success looks like for your business. Why is this important? Well, a well-crafted vision statement has the power to attract investors, engage employees, and captivate customers.

**Steps to Craft a Vision Statement:**

1. **Reflect on Your Core Values:** Consider what your startup stands for and what values are non-negotiable. These values should be the cornerstone of your vision.
2. **Think Long-Term:** Envision where you want your business to be in 5, 10, or even 20 years. This isn't about specific goals but rather the broader impact you want to make.
3. **Be Inspirational:** Use language that evokes passion and commitment. Your vision should be ambitious yet attainable, motivating everyone involved to strive for greatness.
4. **Keep It Concise:** A vision statement should be brief and memorable. Aim for one to two sentences that clearly convey your future aspirations.

Let's complete this with another example we will be using later. Imagine you are starting a company focused on sustainable fashion. Your vision statement might be: "To lead the global fashion industry towards a sustainable future, one ethically-made garment at a time."

**Aligning Your Mission with Business Goals**

Now you have the vision, the mission statement is the next step. While your vision statement outlines your ultimate destination, your mission statement describes <u>how you will get there</u>. It defines your purpose and the approach you will take to achieve your vision. Aligning your mission with your business goals ensures that every strategic decision you make supports your overarching objectives.

**Steps to Develop a Mission Statement:**

1. **Define Your Purpose:** Identify the core purpose of your business. What need are you fulfilling? Why does your company exist?
2. **Outline Key Activities:** Describe the primary activities or services your business provides to achieve its purpose.
3. **Identify Your Audience:** Consider who you are serving – your customers, employees, investors, and the community.

4. **Incorporate Core Values:** Ensure that your mission statement reflects the values and principles that are central to your business.

Coming back to the same sustainable fashion company, a mission statement might be: "To create high-quality, ethically-made clothing that reduces environmental impact and promotes fair labor practices, empowering consumers to make conscious fashion choices."

## Communicating Your Vision to the Team

A vision and mission are only effective if <u>they are shared and embraced by your team</u>. This is important.. otherwise you may have the feeling the purpose of the company gets lost somewhere. Clear communication is essential to ensure everyone is aligned and working towards the same goals.

## Strategies to Communicate Your Vision:

1. **Lead by Example:** Demonstrate your commitment to the vision and mission in your actions and decisions. Your behavior sets the tone for the entire team.
2. **Regular Updates:** Incorporate your vision and mission into regular team meetings, updates, and communications. Repetition helps to reinforce these concepts.
3. **Visual Reminders:** Use posters, digital displays, and other visual tools to keep the vision and mission top of mind for everyone in the organization.
4. **Involve the Team:** Encourage team members to share their thoughts on how their roles contribute to the vision. This fosters a sense of ownership and commitment.
5. **Celebrate Milestones:** Acknowledge and celebrate when the team achieves milestones that align with the vision and mission. This reinforces the connection between their efforts and the bigger picture.

> ***Example:***
>
> *Consider holding a company-wide meeting where you share the vision and mission, explain their importance, and discuss how each department's work contributes to these overarching goals. Follow up with smaller team discussions to delve deeper into specific contributions and gather feedback.*

By crafting a compelling vision statement, aligning your mission with business goals, and effectively communicating your vision to your team, you lay a strong foundation for your startup. This clarity and unity of purpose will guide your decisions and actions, helping to navigate the challenges and opportunities ahead, all together!

# 3. BUILDING THE RIGHT TEAM

In this chapter you will find:

- Hiring for Success: Lessons from Big 4 and Beyond
- Embracing Diversity: The Power of a Varied Team
- Assessing Candidates: Beyond Resumes and References

**Hiring for Success: Lessons from Big 4 and Beyond**

When it comes to building a successful startup, one of the most critical steps is hiring the right team. I've seen many founders gravitate towards candidates from the Big 4 consulting firms (Deloitte, PwC, EY, and KPMG - or similar.. you know what I mean - ) because they believe these professionals come with a guaranteed level of experience and skills. These firms have rigorous hiring and training processes, so it makes sense that their alumni are often well-prepared for demanding roles.

However, while Big 4 experience can be a valuable asset, it's not the only indicator of potential success. The startup environment is vastly different from the corporate world. Startups require agility, creativity, and a willingness to wear multiple hats. It's important to look beyond the brand names on a resume and consider whether a candidate has the versatility and entrepreneurial spirit needed to thrive in a dynamic setting.

**Embracing Diversity: The Power of a Varied Team**

A diverse team brings a wealth of perspectives, ideas, and solutions to the table. In the early stages of a startup, every team member's contribution is crucial, and a homogeneous group can quickly fall into groupthink. By embracing diversity in all its forms—gender, ethnicity, background, and experience—you're more likely to build a team that can approach problems from multiple angles and innovate effectively. All my support to gender and ethnicity, these are very important but in this book I would like to highlight background and experience, they will see things you have in front of you that you wouldn't see in years.

Diverse teams are proven to be more creative and better at problem-solving. They challenge each other's assumptions and push for better solutions. Moreover, a varied team can better understand and serve a diverse customer base. When your team reflects the diversity of your target market, you're in a stronger position to meet their needs and exceed their expectations.

### Assessing Candidates: Beyond Resumes and References

Resumes and references provide a snapshot of a candidate's past achievements and skills, but they don't tell the whole story. In a startup, you need people who are not just qualified, but also passionate and aligned with your vision. However, I have to admit that I always start by asking myself three questions: Is this person good-hearted? Will this person cause me trouble? Is this person hardworking? As soon as I realize all three answers are 'yes,' I proceed with the rest; otherwise, there's no need to waste more time. If I proceed, here are some strategies I'm using to assess candidates more holistically:

1. **Behavioral Interviews:** Ask about specific situations where the candidate had to demonstrate creativity, resilience, or teamwork. Behavioral questions can reveal how they handle challenges and whether they have the startup mindset.
2. **Cultural Fit:** Evaluate whether the candidate shares your company's values and vision. This can be gauged through their enthusiasm for your mission and how they interact with your team during the interview process.
3. **Problem-Solving Exercises:** Give candidates real-world problems to solve. This not only tests their skills but also shows you how they approach new challenges and think on their feet.
4. **Trial Periods:** I find this one very relevant for senior roles. If possible, start with a short-term contract or a probationary period.

This gives both you and the candidate a chance to see if it's a good fit without long-term commitment.
5. **Team Interviews:** Involve multiple team members in the interview process to get diverse perspectives on the candidate. This also gives the candidate a better sense of the team dynamics and whether they feel they can contribute positively.

Building the right team is about more than just filling positions, I think it is a piece of art... It's about finding people who are as committed to your startup's success as you are, who bring diverse perspectives and skills, and who can grow with your company. By looking beyond traditional indicators of success and focusing on fit, passion, and potential, you'll be better positioned to build a team that can take your startup to new heights, or at least, maintain the boat floating when needed (which I'm telling you.. be ready because at some point it will happen).

# 4. Creating a Positive Work Environment

In this chapter you will find:

- The Two Pizza Rule: Lessons from Jeff Bezos
- Listening to All Voices: Why Juniors Should Speak First
- Building Trust: Evaluating Compatibility and Integrity

**The Two Pizza Rule: Lessons from Jeff Bezos**

I have to admit that I read as much as I can.. but sometimes I find it difficult to find time. I try to retain as much as possible, but years ago I realized it was impossible, too much meant nothing... Some years ago, I found something that works for me: identifying a couple of key points that are applicable to my day-to-day life and trying to apply them when possible. If you find yourself in a similar situation, I recommend you try it. This is an example of one of them—the Two Pizza Rule from Jeff Bezos.

Creating a positive work environment often starts with the structure of your teams. Jeff Bezos, the founder of Amazon, introduced the "Two Pizza Rule" to ensure teams remain effective and manageable. According to this rule, if a team can't be fed with two pizzas, it's too large. You know.. the startup grows, everybody does everything, so everybody has to be involved.. At this point you realize you are not on the right path. Smaller teams are more agile, communicate better, and can make decisions faster. This approach fosters a sense of intimacy and collaboration, making it easier for team members to connect and work towards common goals. Applying this principle in your startup you will maintain efficiency and cohesiveness as you grow.

**Listening to All Voices: Why Juniors Should Speak First**

In traditional hierarchies, senior members often dominate discussions, which can stifle creativity and discourage junior team members from sharing their ideas. However, some of the most innovative solutions can come from fresh perspectives. Encouraging juniors to speak first can democratize the decision-making process and ensure that all voices are heard. This practice not only boosts morale and engagement but also leads to more diverse and innovative solutions. We could write pages about practices and methods for making this happen.. but I suggest you do like me, just ask. Period.

**Building Trust: Evaluating Compatibility and Integrity**

Trust is the cornerstone of any positive work environment. It begins with hiring individuals who not only have the right skills but also align with your company's values and culture. Do your homework when hiring; evaluating compatibility and integrity during the hiring process is crucial. Once you have the right people, fostering an atmosphere of transparency and mutual respect will help maintain that trust. Understand these three pillars and you are all set: transparent communication (avoid toxicity or being misleading), integrity in actions (do and behave as you say and want others to do), and creating a safe space for feedback and collaboration (listen, listen and listen! aggregate data and graphs about eNPS [Employee Net Promoter Score] is OK but not enough, you need to listen to individuals, one by one, be empathic and understand their contributions through these comments).  A disclaimer alert: You will probably realize that replacing the line manager as 90% of execs do when reading the eNPS graphs is not what the team needs..

Note that most of the information you will receive as the company grows will be filtered, there are plenty of things that happen that tell a lot about the individuals you will not know about unless you talk to them. Chat with the concierge, have a coffee with the new intern, have conversations with cleaning service you will go to a second level of knowledge.. ( It may sound silly but I  found out who stole the paper in the office, why our pretty accountant avoided the product dept  as she had an ex there I could then relocate, a new junior with high debt I could support, etc..) Be humble and act always with integrity, they will support you until the end.

As you can imagine I strongly recommend you take care of the employee experience from the onboarding to the offboarding, and not treat him differently when he decides to leave. A great employee experience increases retention and this is key to the success of your business.

The percentage of knowledge lost when an employee leaves can vary widely depending on the type of work, the employee's specialization, and the company's knowledge management practices. However, studies and estimates often place this loss between 70% and 90%.

Here are some factors that influence this percentage:

1. **Level of employee specialization:** An employee with highly specialized or unique knowledge is likely to take away a greater percentage of critical knowledge.
2. **Documentation and knowledge transfer processes:** Companies with robust documentation systems and effective knowledge transfer practices can mitigate the loss. If a company has strong policies for capturing and transferring knowledge, the loss may be lower.
3. **Tenure in the company:** Employees who have been with the company for a longer period typically accumulate more institutional knowledge, and their departure can have a greater impact.
4. **Networks and relationships:** Employees with extensive internal and external networks may take with them tacit knowledge, such as who knows what and how to obtain information.
5. **Type of work:** In highly collaborative jobs, knowledge tends to be more shared, which can reduce the loss compared to more isolated roles.

In summary, while it is challenging to provide an exact percentage applicable to all situations, the loss of knowledge can be significant when an employee leaves unless there are effective mechanisms in place to retain and transfer that knowledge within the organization.

# 5. MASTERING COMMUNICATION AND DECISION-MAKING

In this chapter you will find:

- Effective Communication: The Role of Informal Insights
- Transparent Leadership: Sharing Information and Building Trust
- Making Decisions: Balancing Input and Authority

Effective communication and decision-making are the lifeblood of any successful startup. They are the key elements that ensure alignment, foster a collaborative environment, and drive the organization toward its goals. In this chapter, we will explore the nuances of mastering communication and making sound decisions, emphasizing the importance of informal insights, transparent leadership, and balancing input with authority.

## Effective Communication: The Role of Informal Insights

Communication in a startup goes beyond formal meetings and structured updates. Informal insights, gathered through casual conversations and spontaneous interactions, can provide valuable information that might not surface in more formal settings.

### 1. Encouraging Open Dialogue

Create an environment where employees feel comfortable sharing their thoughts and ideas outside of formal channels. Encourage open dialogue by having informal check-ins, casual team gatherings, and encouraging a culture of approachability. This openness can lead to the discovery of critical insights and foster a sense of belonging among team members. I'm referring to the example I mentioned before about the cleaning service, the concierge, etc.. This is relevant as otherwise the information you are receiving will be filtered and understanding the nuances are important (Alert: This has nothing to do with micromanagement!).

## 2. Leveraging Informal Networks

Identify and leverage the informal networks within your organization. These networks often act as conduits for information that might not reach you through official channels. Engage with employees at all levels and departments, and be attentive to the feedback and observations shared in these informal settings.

## 3. Building Relationships

Strong relationships within the team can enhance communication. Invest time in getting to know your employees personally. Understanding their motivations, strengths, and concerns can help you communicate more effectively and make better-informed decisions.

*Example:*

*Consider a startup where the CEO makes it a point to have lunch with different team members every week. These informal interactions often reveal issues and ideas that would never come up in a boardroom meeting, such as minor process inefficiencies or innovative product suggestions. By fostering these casual conversations, the CEO gains a deeper understanding of the company's dynamics and can address concerns proactively.*

**Transparent Leadership: Sharing Information and Building Trust**

Transparency in leadership is essential for building trust within your team. When leaders are open about the company's goals, challenges, and decision-making processes, it creates a culture of trust and accountability.

## 1. Sharing the Big Picture

Regularly communicate the company's vision, goals, and progress to your team. This helps employees understand how their work contributes to the broader mission and fosters a sense of purpose and direction.

## 2. Being Honest About Challenges

Transparency isn't just about sharing successes; it also involves being honest about challenges and setbacks. When leaders openly discuss difficulties and solicit input on how to overcome them, it can lead to more innovative solutions and a stronger team commitment.

## 3. Encouraging Questions

Create a culture where questioning and feedback are welcomed. When employees feel comfortable asking questions and expressing their concerns, it leads to more robust discussions and better decision-making.

> *Example:*
>
> *In a growing tech startup, the founder holds monthly town hall meetings where all employees are invited to ask questions and discuss the company's progress and challenges. This practice not only keeps everyone informed but also fosters a culture of openness and trust, as employees feel their voices are heard and valued.*

## Making Decisions: Balancing Input and Authority

Effective decision-making in a startup involves finding the right balance between gathering input from the team and exercising executive authority. Both extremes—making decisions unilaterally and relying too heavily on consensus—can be detrimental.

### 1. Seeking Diverse Perspectives

Encourage input from a diverse group of employees. Different perspectives can provide valuable insights and lead to more well-rounded decisions. However, ensure that the process for gathering input is structured to avoid analysis paralysis.

### 2. Setting Clear Decision-Making Roles

Define clear roles and responsibilities for decision-making. While it's important to gather input, it's equally important to know who has the final say. This clarity prevents confusion and ensures decisions are made in a timely manner.

### 3. Communicating Decisions Effectively

Once a decision is made, communicate it clearly to all relevant parties. Explain the reasoning behind the decision and how it aligns with the company's goals. This transparency helps in gaining buy-in and understanding from the team.

> *Example:*
>
> *A startup facing a critical product launch deadline might involve the entire product team in brainstorming solutions for a technical issue. After gathering ideas and evaluating the options, the CTO makes the final call on the best approach. The CTO then explains the decision to the team, highlighting the factors considered and the expected outcomes. This process ensures that the team's expertise is utilized while maintaining clear leadership and direction.*

## All in all..

Mastering communication and decision-making is crucial for the success of any startup. By fostering open dialogue and leveraging informal insights, practicing transparent leadership, and balancing input with authority in decision-making, you can build a cohesive, motivated team and make informed, effective decisions. These skills will help you navigate the complexities of startup life, ensuring that your company remains agile, aligned, and ready to tackle any challenge.

# Part II: Managing Growth and Challenges

## 6. Avoiding Common Pitfalls

> In this chapter you will find:
>
> - Scope Creep: Staying Focused on Value
> - Managing Expectations: Avoiding Overpromises
> - Diversifying Client Base: The Risks of Single-Client Dependency

**Scope Creep: Staying Focused on Value**

If you ever have been in project management you probably know about Scope Creep. It is one of the most insidious challenges in this discipline. This occurs when the scope of a project gradually expands beyond its original objectives without corresponding increases in resources, time, or budget. It's easy to get excited about additional features or improvements, especially when stakeholders are enthusiastic about new ideas. However, each added feature or change can dilute the original vision and delay the project's completion.

To combat scope creep, it's essential to maintain a clear and focused project scope from the outset. Define what success looks like for the project and ensure that all team members and stakeholders are aligned with these goals. Implement a formal change management process where any new requests or changes are evaluated for their impact on the project's objectives, timeline, and resources. By staying disciplined and focused on delivering value, you can keep the project on track and ensure that additional work doesn't compromise the overall goals.

What does it mean for your startup? Well you can imagine.. do what your customers are willing to pay for, no time for the beauty. I'm going to tell you a secret, this is extremely difficult.. your engineers, designers, etc.. will get excited by their "new baby", they will put time and effort, even outside their working hours to make something outstanding. *Look, the customer only wanted to push a button to get a taxi, not a taxi approaching in 3D, there will be time for this in the future (or not.. will see..).*

## Managing Expectations: Avoiding Overpromises

Another common pitfall is overpromising. In the excitement of winning new clients or impressing stakeholders, it's tempting to commit to ambitious timelines or deliverables. However, making promises that you can't keep can damage your credibility and strain relationships with clients and partners.

To avoid this, be realistic about what you can deliver and by when. Set clear and achievable goals, and communicate openly about the potential challenges and limitations. It's better to underpromise and overdeliver than to set expectations too high and fall short. Regularly update clients and stakeholders on progress and any changes to timelines or deliverables. Transparency builds trust and helps manage expectations more effectively, ensuring that everyone remains on the same page and satisfied with the results.

We all need capital, we need to show we will keep the cash burn rate low and will get these major contracts with these big players. But look at this modeled spreadsheet with these deals displayed and outstanding growth.. you are overpromising and this.. this will come back to you in the future.. as an underperformer? lack of trust? toxic positivity? I always remember my Spanish friend telling me " *Vale más pájaro en mano que cien volando*" which means "A bird in the hand is worth more than a hundred flying". Share reality and expectations, not impossible dreams.

## Diversifying Client Base: The Risks of Single-Client Dependency

Relying heavily on a single client or a few clients for the majority of your revenue is risky. While it might seem advantageous to focus all efforts on securing and maintaining a few large contracts, this dependency can leave your startup vulnerable to significant financial instability if you lose one of these key clients.

Diversification is crucial to mitigating this risk. Develop a strategy to expand your client base and reduce dependency on any single client. This could involve targeting different market segments, exploring new geographic areas, or offering a broader range of services. Building a diverse client portfolio helps to stabilize revenue streams and provides a buffer against market fluctuations or client-specific issues. Additionally, a varied client base can lead to new opportunities and insights, further strengthening your business.

# 7. FINANCIAL MANAGEMENT AND RESOURCE ALLOCATION

In this chapter you will find:

- The Importance of Cash Flow Management
- Understanding Cost of Capital and Financial Risks
- Handling Liabilities: Managing Debt and Financial Obligations

**The Importance of Cash Flow Management**

Cash flow is the lifeblood of any business. It represents the movement of money into and out of your business and affects your ability to cover expenses, invest in growth, and weather financial challenges. Proper cash flow management ensures that you have enough liquidity to meet your obligations and avoid disruptions in your operations. In a startup you will create a dashboard full of KPIs and cash flow related should be #1. Some may say that #1 should be sales related. My friends, without a sale your start up probably lives a few days, without cash you may have serious trouble. The point here is you clearly need to understand how cash flows through your organization. This is not just a picture of cash position at month end, this is how much cash you are burning, how much you are receiving and how much you need to keep the business up and running (Finance folks call it Working Capital).

To manage cash flow effectively, start by creating a detailed cash flow forecast. This involves estimating your expected income and expenses over a specific period. Regularly compare your forecasts with actual cash flow to identify discrepancies and adjust your plans accordingly. Implement strategies to improve cash flow, such as optimizing your accounts receivable process, negotiating better payment terms with suppliers, and monitoring your expenses closely. Maintaining a cash reserve for unexpected expenses or downturns can also provide a critical safety net. What I found out that really works is to link some items in the budget to sales objectives, so, if no sales come in, no expenses in that category can be used. For example, no matter what we pay salaries, however, unless the sales team reaches USD 1M in revenue this month, a new subsidiary in Australia will not be open yet.

## Understanding Cost of Capital and Financial Risks

The cost of capital refers to the expense incurred to obtain funding for your business, whether through equity or debt. Understanding this concept is vital for making informed financial decisions and evaluating investment opportunities. The cost of capital impacts your financial strategy and affects decisions on financing, investments, and operations.

Different sources of capital come with varying costs and implications. Equity financing, such as venture capital or angel investments, may dilute your ownership but make sure you can provide valuable resources and support. Debt financing, such as loans or credit lines, requires regular repayments and interest but allows you to retain full ownership of your business. Evaluate the trade-offs between these options based on your business needs and growth strategy. My personal opinion is that new entrepreneurs tend to give away equity easily where in most of the cases they should be looking for alternative ways of receiving cash. Equity should be either because the investor is strategic and will drastically foster your business or you are almost dead. If you have a business with a demonstrated cash generation model and no investor can make you grow exponentially due to her contacts, capacities, portfolio synergies or market knowledge, then look for loans and credit lines.

In addition to the cost of capital, it's essential to understand the financial risks associated with your business. These can include market risks, credit risks, and operational risks. Develop a risk management plan to identify potential risks and implement strategies to mitigate them. This could involve diversifying revenue streams, securing insurance, or setting up contingency plans.

## Handling Liabilities: Managing Debt and Financial Obligations

Managing liabilities is a critical aspect of financial management. Liabilities include all the debts and financial obligations your business must meet. As you have just seen, in some cases debt (liability) may be good, but this has other side effects.

Start by keeping a detailed record of all your liabilities, including loans, leases, and outstanding payments. Regularly review these obligations to ensure you're meeting repayment schedules and managing interest costs effectively. Consider strategies to manage and reduce debt, such as refinancing high-interest loans, consolidating debt, or negotiating better terms with creditors.

It's also important to strike a balance between leveraging debt for growth and maintaining financial stability. Excessive debt can strain your cash flow and increase financial risk, while conservative use of debt can provide the necessary capital for expansion without overburdening your business. There is even more. When you increase debt you increase your obligations in the balance sheet… and your finance department will encounter difficulties in some common operations. For example, most businesses need credit cards. In order to get credit cards, banks and/or credit card providers will request the balance sheet to perform a risk assessment. Here the problem of having loans, you will be seen as risky and you will probably not get credit cards (note there is a quite good workaround with prepaid virtual debit cards but not always an option…) so again, find a good balance between debt and growth to keep a balance sheet that allow smooth operations for the company.

# 8. Strategic Planning and Execution

> In this chapter you will find:
>
> - Regular SWOT Analysis: Keeping Your Strategy Updated
> - Balancing Quality, Time, and Cost: Choosing Two
> - Location Matters: Strategic Decisions for Growth

Strategic planning and execution are essential for steering your startup toward long-term success. By mastering the following elements, you'll be better equipped to navigate challenges and capitalize on opportunities as you grow your business.

**Regular SWOT Analysis: Keeping Your Strategy Updated**

A SWOT analysis (Strengths, Weaknesses, Opportunities, and Threats) is a powerful tool for assessing your startup's position and guiding your strategic planning. Conducting a SWOT analysis regularly helps you stay aware of internal and external factors that can impact your business. It's not a one-time exercise but a continuous process that should evolve with your business environment.

**Strengths**: Identify what your startup does well. This could include unique skills, proprietary technology, or strong customer relationships. Leverage these strengths to differentiate your business from competitors and capitalize on your advantages.

**Weaknesses**: Acknowledge areas where your startup may be lacking. These could be resource constraints, skill gaps, or operational inefficiencies. Understanding your weaknesses allows you to address them proactively and seek improvements.

**Opportunities**: Look for external factors that could benefit your startup. This might involve emerging market trends, technological advancements, or changes in consumer behavior. Position your startup to take advantage of these opportunities by aligning your strategy with market demands.

**Threats**: Be aware of potential risks that could negatively impact your business. This could include competitive pressures, economic downturns, or regulatory changes. Develop strategies to mitigate these threats and protect your business from adverse effects.

By regularly updating your SWOT analysis, you can keep your strategic plan relevant and responsive to changes in your business landscape. Here is the relevant point, the work doesn't finish here, once the SWOT is completed/updated work on your key points of differentiation (what makes us different from the rest? why to choose us?) and finally build a positioning map. That's it.. most of the cases this is what you need, even though some will insist you need expensive consulting firms to produce "magical" slides, please make sure these are useful at your stage. Consultancy firms have plenty of knowledge and can be extremely useful, but from my experience, sometimes they are used when not needed and the other way around.

**Balancing Quality, Time, and Cost: Choosing Two**

Let's come back to project management for a second. In the world of project management and strategic execution, the concept of balancing quality, time, and cost is crucial. Often referred to as the project management triangle, it's a principle that emphasizes that you can only achieve two of these three factors at a time.

1. **Quality and Time**: If you prioritize high quality and fast delivery, you may need to <u>increase costs</u>. This could involve investing in top-notch resources or expediting production processes to meet tight deadlines while maintaining quality.

   > *Example: The Launch of an iPhone Model*
   >
   > ***Scenario***: *Apple is known for its high-quality products and its ability to release new models quickly. When Apple prepares to launch a new*

31

> iPhone, they prioritize both high quality and fast delivery. This involves substantial investment in top-notch materials, cutting-edge technology, and a highly skilled workforce. The production process is expedited with advanced manufacturing techniques and close collaboration with suppliers to ensure that the new iPhone meets Apple's stringent quality standards while hitting the market on time.
>
> **Details**:
>
> - **Investment in Resources**: Apple invests heavily in research and development, as well as in securing high-quality components from various global suppliers.
> - **Expedited Production**: The manufacturing process is carefully planned to meet tight deadlines, often involving overtime or additional shifts to keep production on schedule.

2. **Quality and Cost**: Focusing on high quality while keeping costs low usually requires <u>more time</u>. You may need to invest in thorough research and development or extensive testing, which can extend project timelines but ensures that the final product meets high standards without excessive spending.

   > **Example: Mailchimp**
   >
   > **Scenario**: Mailchimp, an email marketing platform, started as a small startup with a limited budget. To provide a high-quality service while keeping costs under control, Mailchimp focused on delivering essential features and iterating based on user feedback. They prioritized building a reliable and user-friendly product without overextending their financial resources.
   >
   > **Details**:
   >
   > - **Extended Timeline**: Mailchimp took a gradual approach to product development, starting with core features and then

> *refining and expanding its offerings based on user needs and feedback. This iterative process ensured that they did not rush to release a full-featured product prematurely.*
> - ***Cost Efficiency****: The startup utilized cost-effective technologies and a lean development team to keep expenses manageable. They also focused on organic growth through word-of-mouth and referrals, minimizing the need for expensive marketing campaigns. By being judicious with their resources and prioritizing high-impact features, Mailchimp maintained quality while controlling costs.*

3. **Time and Cost**: If you need to deliver quickly and manage costs effectively, you might have to compromise on quality. This approach can help you meet tight deadlines and stay within budget but may result in a product or service that doesn't fully meet your quality expectations.

> ***Example: Fast-Fashion Brands***
>
> ***Scenario****: Fast-fashion brands like Zara or H&M often prioritize rapid delivery and cost management over the highest quality. They produce large volumes of fashion items quickly and at a lower cost to respond to the latest trends. This can sometimes mean that the quality of the garments is compromised in favor of speed and affordability.*
>
> ***Details****:*
> - ***Rapid Production****: These brands use efficient supply chains and production processes to quickly bring new designs to market.*
> - ***Cost Management****: They often use lower-cost materials and streamlined manufacturing techniques to keep production costs down, which may result in a lower quality product*

> *compared to higher-end fashion brands.*

Understanding these trade-offs allows you to make informed decisions about your projects and resources. It's important to align your choices with your business goals and customer expectations to achieve the best possible outcomes. This basic triangle of project management is extremely relevant for strategic planning, make sure you choose one and deploy operations according to configure and organization fully aligned with it..

**Location Matters: Strategic Decisions for Growth**

Location plays a significant role in the success of your startup. Whether you're considering where to base your operations, open new offices, or expand into new markets, strategic location decisions can impact your growth and operational efficiency.

1. **Proximity to Target Market**: Being close to your target market can enhance customer relationships and streamline logistics. It allows you to better understand local preferences and respond quickly to market demands. If you have physical sales points you have to work very locally! Take a look at the area you want to establish, which are the main avenues? Shopping malls? Spend time visiting the area, take a stroll, compare and identify the ideal places. Other type of businesses may have a different approach, just being in a specific city close to the business area could be enough
2. **Access to Talent**: Consider the availability of skilled talent in your chosen location. Setting up in an area with a strong pool of professionals in your industry can facilitate recruitment and support your team's growth. Don't forget remote work policies are usually in place to mitigate or eliminate this specific point.
3. **Cost of Operations**: Analyze the cost implications of different locations, including rent, utilities, and local taxes. Balancing these costs with the benefits of the location will help you make informed decisions that align with your budget and financial goals.

4. **Regulatory Environment**: Different locations have varying regulations and business climates. Evaluate how local laws, regulations, and business practices might affect your startup and choose locations that align with your operational needs.
5. **Logistics and Supply Chain**: Proximity to suppliers, distribution centers, and transportation networks can impact your efficiency and costs. Choose locations that facilitate smooth logistics and minimize supply chain disruptions.

Strategic location decisions should be made with careful consideration of these factors to support your startup's growth and operational success.

# 9. BUILDING A STRONG SALES STRATEGY

> In this chapter you will find:
>
> - Developing a Solid Sales Team vs. Relying on Personal Contacts
> - The Realities of Sales Forecasts: Understanding Their Limits
> - Evaluating Business Models: Creation vs. Manufacturing

A robust sales strategy is crucial for the growth and sustainability of any startup. While personal contacts can give you a quick start, a solid sales team is essential for long-term success. Understanding the limitations of sales forecasts and evaluating different business models are also key components of building a strong sales strategy.

**Developing a Solid Sales Team vs. Relying on Personal Contacts**

When you first launch your startup, leveraging personal contacts can be a valuable way to gain initial traction. That should be it. Relying solely on these contacts can limit your growth potential. To scale your business, you need to develop a solid sales team, otherwise you will be dead. A strong executive with great personal contacts can make deals at the beginning but in my experience it doesn't mean the startup grows because there is market traction, there could be several other reasons.

**The Power of Personal Contacts**

Personal contacts can provide a quick entry into the market. They can open doors to early opportunities, help you build initial credibility, and provide valuable feedback. However, this approach has its limitations:

1. **Limited Reach**: Your network can only extend so far. Once you've exhausted your personal contacts, growth can stall.
2. **Lack of Structure**: Relying on informal relationships can lead to inconsistent sales processes and outcomes.
3. **Sustainability**: Personal contacts may not always be reliable or available, making it difficult to sustain growth over time.

**Building a Solid Sales Team**

A solid sales team is the backbone of a sustainable sales strategy. Here's how to build one:

1. **Hiring the Right People**: Look for individuals with proven sales experience, a strong work ethic, and excellent communication skills. This proven experience should be in your industry otherwise it may be worth nothing. Diversity in your sales team can bring different perspectives and approaches, which can be a significant advantage.
2. **Training and Development**: Invest in continuous training to ensure your sales team is up-to-date with the latest sales techniques and product knowledge. Regular training sessions can improve their skills and boost their confidence.
3. **Establishing Processes**: Develop standardized sales processes to ensure consistency and efficiency. This includes defining sales stages, creating scripts for different scenarios, and using a CRM system to manage customer relationships. My quick recommendation here is to prepare a sales funnel at the beginning and that's it.. many will complain about the process but the truth is most of the cases they will not be pointing to the root cause. If you don't sell it can be the sales approach, the value proposition or the market fit, the process will be needed but please, sell stuff first to prove your business model.
4. **Setting Clear Goals**: Establish clear, achievable sales targets and metrics to measure performance. Regularly review these targets and adjust them as necessary to keep your team motivated and focused. Ensure these goals are consistent across the organization. This is very relevant! I've been in places where the CEO due to promises and needs of capital rise was insisting on keeping USD 25M of revenue in the model, the Chief Commercial officer explaining openly that will only make USD 13M and finance due to this being unable to work. Finance was unable to have a unique and trustable model to be shared with everybody and was totally unable to provide clear and concise information on basics like cash forecast positions. One view for everybody. All in the same boat, rowing together, towards the same goal. Period.

5. **Providing Support**: Ensure your sales team has the resources they need, such as marketing materials, product information, and technical support. Encourage open communication and provide regular feedback to help them improve.

> *Example: Salesforce*
>
> *Salesforce, a leader in cloud-based software, attributes much of its success to its strong sales team. Marc Benioff, the founder, focused on building a robust sales force from the beginning. By hiring experienced salespeople and providing them with extensive training and resources, Salesforce was able to scale rapidly and dominate the market.*

## The Realities of Sales Forecasts: Understanding Their Limits

Sales forecasts are essential for planning and decision-making, but they are not always accurate. Understanding their limitations can help you make better-informed decisions and avoid potential pitfalls.

### The Importance of Sales Forecasts

1. **Planning**: Sales forecasts help you plan for production, staffing, and inventory management. They provide a roadmap for future growth and resource allocation.
2. **Budgeting**: Accurate forecasts are crucial for budgeting and financial planning. They help you anticipate revenue and manage expenses.
3. **Investor Confidence**: Investors rely on sales forecasts to gauge the potential success of your startup. Reliable forecasts can boost investor confidence and attract funding.

### Understanding the Limits of Sales Forecasts

1. **Uncertainty**: Sales forecasts are based on assumptions and predictions, which can be affected by various factors such as market

conditions, competition, and economic changes. Unexpected events can significantly impact the accuracy of forecasts.
2. **Bias**: Forecasts can be influenced by optimism or pessimism. Sales teams may overestimate potential sales to meet targets or underestimate them to ensure they exceed expectations.
3. **Data Quality**: The accuracy of sales forecasts depends on the quality of the data used. Incomplete or outdated data can lead to inaccurate predictions.

**Strategies for Improving Sales Forecasts**

1. **Use Multiple Methods**: Combine different forecasting methods, such as historical analysis, market research, and customer feedback, to improve accuracy.
2. **Regular Updates**: Continuously update your forecasts based on the latest data and market conditions. Regular reviews can help you adjust your strategy and stay on track.
3. **Scenario Planning**: Develop different scenarios for best-case, worst-case, and most likely outcomes. This approach can help you prepare for various possibilities and make more resilient plans. Be honest. No, seriously, be honest when creating this model. This is not a document to secure more capital; this is a model for decision-making.

---

*Example: Amazon*

*Amazon uses sophisticated algorithms and machine learning to improve its sales forecasts. By analyzing vast amounts of data, Amazon can make more accurate predictions and adjust its strategies accordingly. This approach has helped Amazon maintain its competitive edge and manage its complex supply chain effectively.*

## Evaluating Business Models: Creation vs. Manufacturing

Choosing the right business model is critical for your startup's success. Two common models are creation (developing your own products or services) and manufacturing (producing goods for other companies). Each has its advantages and challenges.

### Creation Model

In the creation model, you develop and sell your own products or services. This approach allows you to control the entire process, from design to marketing.

**Advantages**:

1. **Brand Control**: You have full control over your brand and product quality. This can help you build a strong, recognizable brand.
2. **Higher Margins**: Developing your own products can result in higher profit margins, as you eliminate intermediaries.
3. **Innovation**: You can continuously innovate and improve your products based on customer feedback and market trends.

**Challenges**:

1. **Higher Costs**: Developing and marketing your own products can be expensive, requiring significant investment in research, development, and marketing.
2. **Risk**: There is a higher risk involved, as you need to ensure there is sufficient demand for your products… and stock management doesn't become a nightmare.

### Manufacturing Model

In the manufacturing model, you produce goods for other companies. This approach focuses on efficiency and volume.

**Advantages**:

1. **Steady Revenue**: Manufacturing contracts can provide a steady stream of revenue, reducing financial uncertainty.
2. **Lower Marketing Costs**: Since you are producing for other companies, you don't need to invest heavily in marketing and branding.
3. **Scalability**: Manufacturing can be scaled up relatively easily to meet increased demand.

**Challenges**:

1. **Lower Margins**: Profit margins in manufacturing can be lower, as you are competing primarily on price. You know what happens when you compete on price.. a never ending process of continuous push downs.
2. **Dependency**: Your business is dependent on the success and demand of the companies you manufacture for. Changes in their business can directly impact you.

---

**Example: Apple**

Apple combines both models effectively. It designs and creates its own products, like the iPhone and MacBook, which allows it to control its brand and maintain high-profit margins. At the same time, Apple outsources manufacturing to companies like Foxconn, which specializes in large-scale production. This combination allows Apple to innovate and maintain quality while managing costs efficiently.

# Part III: Navigating the Entrepreneurial Journey

## 10. Learning from Failures and Mistakes

> In this chapter you will find:
> - Embracing Early Failures: Learning Fast and Cheap
> - Preparing for Setbacks: Emotional and Financial Readiness

In the entrepreneurial journey, failures and mistakes are not just inevitable—they're invaluable. Embracing these experiences and learning from them can be the difference between eventual success and giving up too soon.

**Embracing Early Failures: Learning Fast and Cheap**

Failure often carries a heavy stigma, but in the startup world, it's a badge of honor. The key is to fail early, fail fast, and fail cheap. Early failures are like feedback from the market, telling you what doesn't work so you can pivot quickly. A classic example is to present product concepts, mock designs and other early stage development assets to a diverse audience before moving forward with expensive developments. In my past experience on several occasions this approach saved us thousands of dollars and plenty of time.

> *Example: Buffer's Failed Side Projects*
>
> *Buffer, the social media management tool, didn't hit gold with every idea they pursued. They experimented with several side projects that didn't pan out. Instead of viewing these as wasted efforts, Buffer's team saw them as learning opportunities. Each failure provided insights that informed their*

> *main product's development, ultimately leading to a stronger, more focused offering.*

**How to Embrace Early Failures:**

1. **Experiment Boldly**: Don't be afraid to test new ideas, even if they seem risky. The sooner you try, the sooner you'll know if it's viable.
2. **Measure and Analyze**: Collect data from your experiments. Understand why something didn't work to avoid repeating the same mistakes.
3. **Iterate Quickly**: Use the insights gained to make rapid adjustments. The faster you pivot, the less costly your mistakes become.

**Preparing for Setbacks: Emotional and Financial Readiness**

While embracing failure is important, it's equally crucial to be prepared for setbacks—both emotionally and financially. Entrepreneurship can be a rollercoaster ride, and resilience is key to staying on track.

**Emotional Readiness**

The emotional toll of running a startup can be significant. Rejections, lost deals, and unexpected hurdles can wear you down. Being emotionally prepared means acknowledging that setbacks are part of the journey and developing strategies to cope with them. My personal take on this is to work on yourself to show strength in front of the team; there is nothing worse than a senior leader unable to show confidence. Do not confuse this with toxic positivity. Toxic positivity destroys culture and can ultimately harm the organization.

**Strategies for Emotional Readiness:**

1. **Build a Support Network**: Surround yourself with mentors, fellow entrepreneurs, and supportive friends and family who understand your journey and can offer guidance and encouragement.
2. **Practice Self-Care**: Ensure you're taking care of your mental and physical health. Regular exercise, adequate sleep, and mindfulness practices can help you stay resilient. This is important and is usually the first thing we forget in turbulent times.
3. **Celebrate Small Wins**: Don't wait for the big successes to celebrate. Recognize and appreciate the small victories along the way to maintain motivation and positivity.

**Financial Readiness:**

Financial setbacks can be particularly daunting, but planning and prudent management can help you navigate through tough times.

**Strategies for Financial Readiness:**

1. **Maintain a Cash Reserve**: Set aside funds to cover unexpected expenses or periods of low revenue. A safety net can give you the breathing room to make strategic decisions without the pressure of immediate financial strain.
2. **Monitor Your Finances Closely**: Keep a close eye on your cash flow and budget. Understanding your financial health at all times allows you to make informed decisions and take corrective action when needed.
3. **Diversify Income Streams**: Relying on a single source of revenue can be risky. Explore multiple income streams to buffer against financial setbacks.

*Example: Airbnb's Early Financial Struggles*

*Airbnb faced significant financial challenges in its early days. To stay afloat, the founders sold custom cereal boxes during the 2008 presidential election, raising $30,000. This creative approach provided them with the necessary funds to keep the business going until they secured their first round of funding. Their story underscores the importance of financial resilience and creativity in overcoming setbacks.*

## 11. Legal and Compliance Issues

> In this chapter you will find:
>
> - Protecting Intellectual Property
> - Navigating Regulatory Requirements
> - Building a Strong Legal Foundation

Navigating the legal landscape is crucial for any startup and you as an executive should be aware of some basics related to your industry (Personal health records for digital health startups, IP protection for innovative companies, etc.. ). Properly managing legal and compliance issues protects your business from potential risks and ensures its long-term success. Here,, we will explore the importance of protecting intellectual property, understanding and adhering to regulatory requirements, and building a strong legal foundation for your startup.

**Protecting Intellectual Property**

Intellectual property (IP) is one of the most valuable assets of a startup. It includes inventions, designs, brand names, and proprietary processes (otherwise you can suddenly find yourself in a position where some of your intangible assets in your balance sheet are worth nothing and you are technically bankrupt..). Protecting your IP ensures that competitors cannot unfairly benefit from your hard work and innovation.

**Steps to Protect Intellectual Property:**

1. **Identify Your IP:** Determine what aspects of your business qualify as intellectual property. This can include patents, trademarks, copyrights, and trade secrets.
2. **Register Your IP:**
    - **Patents:** Apply for patents to protect inventions and unique processes. This gives you the exclusive right to use, sell, or license your invention. What nobody tells you is patents are

expensive.. and having patents worldwide it is almost impossible in a startup. My recommendation is to apply patents to the countries where you will end up operating (for example, for the digital healthcare industry it is quite usual to go to the USA, Europe and APAC). I also recommend externalizing this service to people that know about patents, it shouldn't be expensive and should help you focus on the right stuff for your organization. Once you grow.. that's a different story and you may want to bring this service in-house.
    - **Trademarks:** Register trademarks for your brand name, logo, and other distinctive signs that identify your products or services.
    - **Copyrights:** Secure copyrights for original works of authorship such as software code, marketing materials, and website content.
    - **Trade Secrets:** Protect proprietary information that gives your business a competitive edge. Implement confidentiality agreements and secure data storage practices.
3. **Monitor and Enforce Your Rights:** Regularly monitor the market for potential infringements and take legal action when necessary to enforce your IP rights. Don't forget to work on renewals...

---

*Example:*

A tech startup developing a new software platform should patent unique algorithms, register the company name and logo as trademarks, and copyright the software code and user manuals. By doing so, the company can prevent competitors from copying their innovative solutions and capitalize on their intellectual property.

**It is not just patents..**

To close this section please take into account you will have to make a decision on what to protect and what not to protect. When you decide to protect something you will have to decide how strong this protection you want it to be. Patents are great but involve quite a bit of time and resources. Other than patents I found out a second level of protection that worked really well for us; on a quarterly basis we gather all relevant slides produced, new code, etc.. and we then go to a public notary, sign it and archive it. This will demonstrate any time in the future that at that point in time we were working on something or we had some knowledge on a specific topic. As a way of process improvement, we recently changed it and we upload it to a digital signature platform (such as Docusign), sign it yourself and get a copy. As you can see here the point is just to have some kind of external validation that something was done. This is not a patent or pretend it to be, it is totally different. However, it works really well for having proof of something being done at a given point in time.

**Navigating Regulatory Requirements**

Every industry is subject to specific regulations and compliance standards. Understanding and adhering to these requirements is essential to avoid legal issues and maintain a good reputation.

**Steps to Navigate Regulatory Requirements:**

1. **Research Industry Regulations:** Identify the key regulatory bodies and compliance standards relevant to your industry. This may include data protection laws, environmental regulations, health and safety standards, and financial reporting requirements. This is something you can outsource as well.
2. **Implement Compliance Policies:** Develop and implement policies and procedures that ensure compliance with relevant regulations. This includes training employees, conducting regular audits, and maintaining accurate records.
3. **Stay Updated:** Regulations can change frequently. Stay informed about any changes in laws and regulations that may impact your

business. Join industry associations, subscribe to legal updates, and consult with legal experts regularly.
4. **Consult with Legal Experts:** Engage legal professionals who specialize in your industry to provide guidance on complex regulatory issues and ensure your business remains compliant.

---

*Example:*

*A healthcare startup must comply with various regulations such as HIPAA (Health Insurance Portability and Accountability Act) in the United States. This involves implementing strict data protection measures, training employees on patient privacy, and regularly auditing systems for compliance. Failure to comply with HIPAA can result in severe penalties and damage to the company's reputation.*

---

## Building a Strong Legal Foundation

Establishing a solid legal foundation from the outset can save your startup from costly legal battles and operational disruptions down the line. This includes structuring your business correctly, drafting essential contracts, and ensuring proper governance.

**Steps to Build a Strong Legal Foundation:**

1. **Choose the Right Business Structure:** Select a business structure that aligns with your goals and provides the necessary legal protections. Options include sole proprietorship, partnership, limited liability company (LLC), and corporation.
2. **Draft Key Contracts:** Create legally binding contracts for various aspects of your business, including:

- **Founders' Agreement:** Outlines the roles, responsibilities, and equity distribution among the founding team.
- **Employment Contracts:** Specifies the terms of employment, including roles, compensation, and confidentiality clauses.
- **Customer and Supplier Contracts:** Clearly define the terms of service, payment, and deliverables to avoid disputes.
- **Non-Disclosure Agreements (NDAs):** Protect sensitive information when dealing with partners, contractors, and potential investors.

For scalability, create contract templates and establish rules for when and how to use them (for example, up to a specific contract value). This approach will provide agility to your organization and allow you or your legal team to focus on more significant matters. Quite useful examples include NDAs for potential investors and NDAs for potential suppliers.

3. **Implement Governance Practices:** Establish clear governance structures and practices to ensure accountability and transparency. This includes regular board meetings, accurate record-keeping, and compliance with corporate governance standards. A standard RACI matrix can be put in place for the contract lifecycle but.. if that's too much just make sure you have somebody with authority responsible for contracts in your organization.
4. **Seek Ongoing Legal Advice:** Engage with legal counsel to review contracts, handle disputes, and provide ongoing legal support as your business grows. Make sure he is truly an expert in your industry..

---

*Example:*

*A startup in the fintech industry should incorporate as a corporation to attract investors and provide limited liability protection. They should draft*

> *comprehensive employment contracts, NDAs, and customer agreements to safeguard their interests. Regular consultations with legal counsel will help navigate complex regulatory environments and ensure ongoing compliance.*

By focusing on protecting intellectual property, navigating regulatory requirements, and building a strong legal foundation, your startup can mitigate risks and set the stage for sustainable growth. Legal and compliance issues may seem daunting, but addressing them proactively will provide peace of mind and allow you to focus on growing your business.

# 12. Customer Relationship Management

> In this chapter you will find:
>
> - Building Strong Customer Relationships
> - Utilizing CRM Tools and Techniques
> - Creating Loyal Customers

## Building Strong Customer Relationships

Building strong customer relationships is foundational to any successful startup. It's key.. because this is what brings revenue... All in all it's more than just a business transaction; it's about forming a connection that encourages trust, loyalty, and continued engagement.

### Understanding Your Customers

Knowing your customers is the first step in building strong relationships. Dive deep into understanding their needs, preferences, and pain points. This is not about pushing your products, this is about providing value to them after an understanding of their needs. Collect feedback through surveys, direct interactions, and social media engagement. The more you know about your customers, the better you can serve them.

### Personalized Experiences

Customers appreciate when businesses go the extra mile to make them feel valued. Use the data you've gathered to personalize their experiences. This can be as simple as using their name in communications or offering recommendations based on their previous purchases. Personalized experiences make customers feel seen and appreciated, enhancing their loyalty.

## Effective Communication

Clear and consistent communication is vital. Keep your customers informed about new products, services, and updates. Be transparent about any changes that might affect them. Always try to respond promptly to their inquiries and address their concerns. If you do not have the answer at that moment, just provide a quick ACK email with an estimate for the full reply. Effective communication fosters trust and shows customers that you value their input.

## Exceptional Customer Service

Outstanding customer service can set your business apart. Train your team to handle customer interactions with empathy and professionalism (My recommendation.. as always.. a sales playbook!) . Resolve issues swiftly and satisfactorily. A positive customer service experience can turn a frustrated customer into a loyal advocate for your brand.

## Utilizing CRM Tools and Techniques

Customer Relationship Management (CRM) tools are essential for organizing, automating, and synchronizing sales, marketing, and customer service efforts. They help in managing interactions with current and potential customers.

## Choosing the Right CRM System

Selecting the appropriate CRM system is crucial. Look for one that aligns with your business needs, is easy to use, and scalable as your business grows. Some popular CRM systems include Salesforce, HubSpot, and Zoho CRM. Ensure the system can integrate with other tools you use, such as email marketing platforms or customer support systems.

## Centralizing Customer Information

A CRM system centralizes all customer information, making it accessible to your team. This includes contact details, communication history, purchase history, and preferences. Centralized information ensures that your team is always informed and can provide a consistent customer experience.

## Automating Routine Tasks

CRM systems can automate repetitive tasks like sending follow-up emails, scheduling appointments, and generating reports. Automation saves time and reduces the risk of errors, allowing your team to focus on more strategic activities that enhance customer relationships.

## Data Analysis and Insights

CRM tools offer valuable insights through data analysis. Track customer behavior, identify trends, and measure the effectiveness of your marketing campaigns. Use these insights to refine your strategies and make data-driven decisions. Understanding your customers better through data helps in tailoring your approach to meet their needs effectively.

## Creating Loyal Customers

Loyal customers are the backbone of a successful business. They not only make repeat purchases but also promote your brand through word-of-mouth, attracting new customers.

## Exceeding Expectations

To create loyal customers, consistently exceed their expectations. Deliver quality products and services, and look for opportunities to delight your customers. This could be through unexpected discounts, personalized thank-you notes, or exceptional customer support.

## Regular Engagement

Stay engaged with your customers to keep your brand top-of-mind. Use email newsletters, social media, and loyalty programs to maintain regular contact. Share valuable content, offer exclusive deals, and invite feedback to foster a sense of community.

**Rewarding Loyalty**

Recognize and reward your loyal customers. Implement a loyalty program that offers incentives such as discounts, early access to new products, or special events. Show appreciation for their continued support and contributions to your business.

**Building Trust**

Trust is the cornerstone of customer loyalty. Be transparent, honor your commitments, and handle customer data responsibly. Building trust takes time but is essential for creating a loyal customer base.

**All in all...**

We could write an entire book about this.. and I tried just to provide insights and keep it short. Effective customer relationship management is about more than just managing interactions; it's about building strong, lasting connections with your customers. By understanding their needs, utilizing CRM tools, and fostering loyalty, you can create a loyal customer base that supports the long-term success of your startup. Remember, a satisfied and loyal customer is one of your most valuable assets.

# 13. DELEGATION AND LEADERSHIP

> In this chapter you will find:
>
> - The Power of Delegation: Avoiding Decision Bottlenecks
> - Simplifying Processes: Avoiding Overcomplication

In the realm of startups and growing businesses, the concepts of delegation and leadership are paramount. Effective delegation can significantly enhance productivity and efficiency, while strong leadership ensures the team remains cohesive and motivated.

**The Power of Delegation: Avoiding Decision Bottlenecks**

Delegation is more than just assigning tasks to others; it is about empowering your team and leveraging their strengths to achieve common goals. As a startup founder or a leader, you might be tempted to retain control over all aspects of your business. However, this approach can lead to burnout and hinder your company's growth. Delegation, when done effectively, can prevent decision bottlenecks and distribute workload evenly, allowing for more agile and responsive business operations.

**Understanding the Need for Delegation**

Every leader must recognize that they cannot do everything themselves. Trying to handle every detail personally not only slows down decision-making but also stifles the potential of your team members. When you delegate, you are not just offloading tasks; you are trusting your team to take ownership and responsibility. This builds their confidence, improves their skills, and enhances overall productivity.

> ***Example: Steve Jobs at Apple***
>
> *As you probably already know, Steve Jobs, the co-founder of Apple, was known for his visionary leadership. However, he also understood the importance of delegation. He entrusted key responsibilities to talented individuals like Tim Cook, who handled operations, and Jony Ive, who was responsible for design. This delegation allowed him to focus on his strengths—innovation and product development—while ensuring that other crucial areas of the business were in capable hands.*

**Strategies for Effective Delegation**

1. **Identify Tasks to Delegate**: Start by listing all the tasks you handle daily. Identify which of these tasks can be done by someone else. Focus on delegating tasks that are time-consuming but do not necessarily require your specific expertise.
2. **Choose the Right People**: Match tasks with team members who have the necessary skills and strengths. Ensure they understand the task and have the resources needed to complete it effectively.
3. **Set Clear Expectations**: Clearly communicate the desired outcomes, deadlines, and any specific guidelines. Provide context for why the task is important and how it fits into the bigger picture.
4. **Provide Support and Resources**: Ensure your team has the tools and support they need. Be available to answer questions and provide guidance without micromanaging.
5. **Trust Your Team**: Once you delegate a task, trust your team to handle it. Avoid the urge to micromanage, as this can undermine their confidence and autonomy.
6. **Review and Provide Feedback**: After the task is completed, review the results and provide constructive feedback. Recognize and celebrate successes, and discuss areas for improvement.

## Avoiding Decision Bottlenecks

One of the main advantages of effective delegation is the avoidance of decision bottlenecks. When too many decisions depend on a single person, progress can slow to a crawl and, trust me, this kills creativity and empowerment and ultimately ends up killing the company. By delegating decision-making authority to competent team members, you can ensure that your business remains nimble and responsive.

> ### *Example: Jeff Bezos at Amazon*
>
> *Jeff Bezos, the founder of Amazon, implemented a principle known as "disagree and commit." This principle encourages team members to express their opinions, even if they disagree with the leader's decision. Once a decision is made, everyone commits to it fully. This approach reduces bottlenecks by fostering a culture where decisions can be made quickly and efficiently, without endless debates and delays.*

## Simplifying Processes: Avoiding Overcomplication

As your startup grows, it's easy to fall into the trap of overcomplicating processes. While structure and processes are essential for scalability, overly complex procedures can hinder agility and innovation. Simplifying processes ensures that your team can work efficiently and focus on what truly matters. However, be prepared to filter opinions. No matter what, even with the best processes, there will always be somebody complaining about something.

### The Dangers of Overcomplication

Overcomplicated processes can lead to several issues:

- **Reduced Efficiency**: Complex procedures can slow down work, making it difficult to respond quickly to changes or opportunities.
- **Increased Errors**: The more steps and requirements in a process, the higher the likelihood of mistakes. Thus, you need to find a balance.
- **Lower Morale**: Employees can become frustrated with cumbersome procedures, leading to decreased job satisfaction and productivity.

---

*Example: Google's Innovation Approach*

*Google, known for its innovative culture, emphasizes simplicity in its processes. They encourage employees to spend a portion of their time on projects they are passionate about (known as the "20% time" policy). This simple approach has led to the creation of some of Google's most successful products, such as Gmail and AdSense. By keeping processes straightforward, Google fosters creativity and agility.*

---

## Strategies to Simplify Processes

1. **Map Out Current Processes**: Document your existing processes in detail. Identify steps that are redundant or overly complex.
2. **Focus on Core Objectives**: Ensure that every step in your process aligns with your core objectives. Remove any steps that do not add significant value.
3. **Leverage Technology**: Use technology and automation to streamline processes. Tools like project management software, CRM systems, and automation tools can simplify tasks and reduce manual work. However, be aware that adding a new tool means more work (maintenance, payments, user management, etc..) so I always start by looking at what I already have available in the company.

4. **Empower Teams**: Encourage your teams to take ownership of their processes. Involve them in identifying inefficiencies and brainstorming solutions.
5. **Regularly Review and Adapt**: Continuously review your processes and be open to making changes. As your business evolves, your processes should too.
6. **Pilot and Iterate**: Before fully implementing a simplified process, pilot it with a small team or project. Gather feedback, make necessary adjustments, and then roll it out more broadly.

---

*Example: Lean Startup Methodology*

*The Lean Startup methodology, popularized by Eric Ries, emphasizes the importance of simplicity and iteration. Startups are encouraged to build minimal viable products (MVPs), test them quickly, and iterate based on feedback. This approach avoids the complexity of building fully-featured products that may not meet market needs. By focusing on simple, testable ideas, startups can learn quickly and adapt their strategies.*

# 14. Maintaining Personal Well-Being

In this chapter you will find:

- Work-Life Balance: Finding Life Beyond Work
- Health and Fitness: Its Role in Entrepreneurial Success
- Planning for the Future: Preparing for Potential Exits

In the fast-paced world of startups, maintaining personal well-being often takes a back seat. The demands of building and growing a business can be all-consuming, leading many entrepreneurs to neglect their health, relationships, and long-term happiness. However, personal well-being is crucial for sustained success.

**Work-Life Balance: Finding Life Beyond Work**

Work-life balance is a term that is often thrown around, but its importance cannot be overstated. As an entrepreneur, it's easy to blur the lines between work and personal life. However, failing to establish boundaries can lead to burnout, strained relationships, and decreased productivity. Remember that time is finite, and it is your responsibility to take care of yourself. This starts with ensuring you have the time to recharge, feel well, spend time with friends, and enjoy healthy food. Remember that someday, even if it's in the end, your body will pay the price.

**The Importance of Work-Life Balance**

1. **Preventing Burnout**: Continuous work without adequate rest and relaxation can lead to physical and mental exhaustion. Burnout not only affects your health but also your ability to make sound business decisions.
2. **Enhancing Productivity**: A balanced life allows you to return to work refreshed and with a clear mind, increasing your efficiency and creativity.

3. **Improving Relationships**: Spending quality time with family and friends nurtures your personal relationships, providing emotional support and stability.

---

*Example: Sheryl Sandberg*

*Sheryl Sandberg, COO of Facebook, is known for her advocacy of work-life balance. She leaves work at 5:30 PM every day to have dinner with her children. By setting this boundary, she ensures she dedicates time to her family, which in turn, helps her maintain her energy and focus at work.*

---

**Real-World Strategies for Achieving Work-Life Balance**

1. **Set Boundaries**: Establish clear work hours and stick to them. Communicate these boundaries to your team to ensure they respect your personal time.
2. **Prioritize Tasks**: Focus on high-impact tasks and delegate whenever possible. Use tools like to-do lists and time management apps to stay organized.
3. **Schedule Personal Time**: Just as you schedule meetings and work tasks, schedule time for exercise, hobbies, and family activities. What works really well for me is to put them directly in my Outlook calendar so no availability is displayed during this period.
4. **Unplug Regularly**: Take breaks from technology and work-related communications to recharge. Designate "no work" zones or times in your home.

## Health and Fitness: Its Role in Entrepreneurial Success

Maintaining physical health is often overlooked in the entrepreneurial hustle, but it plays a critical role in your overall success. Regular exercise, a balanced diet, and sufficient sleep can enhance your physical and mental capabilities, making you more effective as a leader.

### The Benefits of Health and Fitness

1. **Increased Energy Levels**: Regular exercise improves cardiovascular health and stamina, giving you more energy to tackle daily challenges. You have to figure out what works for you, some run marathons… I only need 8 miles a day!
2. **Enhanced Mental Clarity**: Physical activity boosts endorphins and reduces stress, improving your mood and cognitive function.
3. **Resilience to Stress**: A healthy body is better equipped to handle stress, reducing the risk of burnout and mental health issues.

> *Example: Richard Branson*
>
> *Richard Branson, the founder of the Virgin Group, attributes much of his success to his commitment to health and fitness. He starts his day with exercise, whether it's swimming, biking, or playing tennis. This routine helps him maintain high energy levels and a positive outlook.*

### Incorporating Health and Fitness into Your Routine

1. **Schedule Exercise**: Treat exercise as a non-negotiable part of your daily routine. Find physical activities you enjoy and can commit to regularly.
2. **Eat Balanced Meals**: Maintain a diet rich in fruits, vegetables, lean proteins, and whole grains. Avoid excessive caffeine and sugar, which can lead to energy crashes.

3. **Get Adequate Sleep**: Aim for 7-8 hours of sleep per night. Develop a bedtime routine to improve sleep quality, such as reading or meditating before bed.
4. **Manage Stress**: Practice stress-reducing techniques like meditation, yoga, or deep-breathing exercises. Regularly take time off to relax and recharge.

## Planning for the Future: Preparing for Potential Exits

While the day-to-day operations of your startup are critical, it's equally important to think about the long-term future. Planning for potential exits ensures that you have a strategy in place for when it's time to move on from your business, whether through selling, merging, or passing it on to successors. To me this starts by understanding my own capacities and skills. where, when and how I can provide value and be prepared months in advance when it is time to say goodbye.

### The Importance of Exit Planning

1. **Maximizing Value**: Proper planning can help you maximize the value of your business when it's time to sell or merge.
2. **Ensuring Continuity**: Planning for succession ensures that your business can continue to thrive even after you step down.
3. **Financial Security**: An exit strategy provides financial security for you and your family, allowing you to transition smoothly to the next phase of your life.

---

*Example: Sara Blakely*

*Sara Blakely, the founder of Spanx, has always been open about her plans for the future of her company. By preparing for potential exits and involving her team in the planning process, she has ensured that Spanx can continue to grow and innovate even after she steps back from day-to-day operations.*

## Steps to Develop an Exit Strategy

1. **Define Your Goals**: Clarify your personal and financial goals for the future. Determine what you want to achieve with your exit, whether it's retirement, pursuing new ventures, or financial independence.
2. **Evaluate Your Business**: Conduct a thorough assessment of your business's value, including assets, intellectual property, and market position. Seek professional valuation if necessary.
3. **Identify Potential Buyers or Successors**: Determine who might be interested in acquiring your business. This could be competitors, investors, or even key employees.
4. **Create a Succession Plan**: If you plan to pass your business on to a successor, identify and train potential candidates. Ensure they are prepared to take over leadership roles.
5. **Consult Professionals**: Work with financial advisors, attorneys, and business brokers to develop a comprehensive exit strategy. They can provide valuable insights and help you navigate the complexities of the process.

Never forget it's not only about the company, it is also about you. Have some money in your bank account during the transition so you can sleep well or ensure you have another job on the table.

---

*Example: Elon Musk*

*Elon Musk, the CEO of Tesla and SpaceX, has always kept an eye on the future. He ensures that each of his ventures has a clear succession plan and exit strategy, which allows him to focus on innovation while being prepared for any eventuality.*

# Part IV: Future-Proofing Your Startup

## 15. Scaling and Sustaining Growth

> In this chapter you will find:
>
> - Growing Comfortably: Finding Your Growth Limit
> - Building Long-Term Partnerships: Choosing the Right Providers

**Growing Comfortably: Finding Your Growth Limit**

One of the biggest challenges in scaling a startup is knowing how fast to grow. Too slow, and you risk being overtaken by competitors; too fast, and you could stretch your resources too thin, leading to operational issues and potential failure. Finding your growth limit involves understanding the capacity of your team, resources, and infrastructure.

**Assessing Your Capacity**

1. **Team and Talent**: Evaluate your team's ability to handle increased workloads. This includes assessing their skills, experience, and the need for additional hires. A stressed team can lead to burnout and high turnover rates, which can derail growth efforts. At the same time, evaluate yourself! It is not the same as a small startup with 10 people trying to grow compared to the same startup 3+ years later with 200 people. Ask yourself, am I ready for a bigger organization?
2. **Financial Resources**: Ensure you have the financial stability to support growth. This includes having enough capital for new hires, marketing efforts, product development, and other operational expenses. Overextending financially can lead to cash flow issues and potentially jeopardize your business. Managing cash properly is the key!

3. **Operational Infrastructure**: Review your current operational processes and systems. Are they scalable? Do you have the technology and processes in place to handle increased demand? This might involve investing in new technology, upgrading existing systems, or streamlining processes to increase efficiency. Hopefully in most of the cases this will not be necessary. Some tools just have different packages (for example, from 1-10 users, from 11 to 50 users, etc..) so it shouldn't be that difficult. But when necessary this can be painful, a clear example is a startup in the SaaS (Software as a Service) model. Did you prepare the database for 100K+ users before you invested in marketing campaigns? Ask yourself what is needed to support realistic growth expectations before it is too late.

**Setting Realistic Goals**

1. **Short-Term Milestones**: Break down your long-term growth goals into manageable short-term milestones. This allows you to track progress, make adjustments as needed, and celebrate achievements along the way. When possible try to make these work packages with no or minimum dependencies between them! For example, product development creates a login page that for now is functional so the user/password, and private policy are built there. The team moves to other functionalities and when branding has the logo and design ready they come back and apply the beauty.
2. **Adaptability**: Stay flexible and be prepared to adjust your growth strategy based on market conditions, feedback, and internal performance. This adaptability can help you navigate challenges and seize new opportunities as they arise.

---

*Example: Slack*

*Slack, the popular messaging platform, is a prime example of growing comfortably. Initially launched as an internal communication tool for a failed game development project, Slack focused on perfecting their product before scaling. They listened to user feedback, made necessary adjustments,*

> *and only then did they invest in marketing and growth. This measured approach allowed them to grow sustainably and become a dominant player in the communication tools market.*

## Building Long-Term Partnerships: Choosing the Right Providers

Successful scaling often relies on building strong partnerships with providers who can support your growth. Choosing the right providers is crucial for maintaining quality, ensuring reliability, and fostering long-term success. From my point of view, some key areas and functions shouldn't use providers, they should instead partner. For example, you outsource accounting to a Big 4 company, you rather want your time to work with them on a daily basis, adapting and discussing to produce accurate numbers rather than just getting monthly reports with unclear dimension misalignments.

### Identifying Potential Partners

1. **Reputation and Reliability**: Research potential partners thoroughly. Look for those with a solid reputation and a track record of reliability. This can include suppliers, technology providers, logistics companies, and more. Check reviews, request references, and conduct due diligence to ensure they can meet your needs.
2. **Scalability**: Ensure your partners can scale with you. As your business grows, you'll need partners who can handle increased volumes and demands without compromising on quality or service. My recommendation is to produce some what-if scenarios based on the information you have for the mid and long-term plans and see how they can support you. For example, paying a little more for a partner with international offices in countries you plan to set up in the future can support you in your international growth.
3. **Alignment of Values**: Choose partners whose values align with your own. This alignment can foster a more collaborative and productive

relationship, ensuring both parties are working towards the same goals.

## Building Strong Relationships

1. **Clear Communication**: Establish open and transparent communication channels with your partners (at all levels!). This includes setting clear expectations, regularly reviewing performance, and addressing any issues promptly.
2. **Mutual Benefits**: Aim for partnerships that offer mutual benefits. This can involve negotiating terms that are favorable for both parties, ensuring a win-win situation. Long-term partnerships are more sustainable when both sides feel valued and appreciated. There will be occasions they may ask you to collaborate on some kind of public exhibitions or presentations, say yes! It may be just a small thing for you but will create stronger links between both.
3. **Regular Reviews**: Conduct regular reviews of your partnerships to ensure they continue to meet your needs (at all levels as well!). This can involve performance assessments, feedback sessions, and strategic planning discussions.

*Example: Apple and Foxconn*

*Apple's partnership with Foxconn is a notable example of a successful long-term relationship. Foxconn, a major electronics manufacturer, has been a key partner for Apple in producing its iPhones and other products. The partnership has been built on mutual benefits: Apple gets high-quality, scalable manufacturing capabilities, while Foxconn benefits from Apple's consistent and substantial demand. This long-term relationship has enabled Apple to scale its production efficiently and maintain its position as a leader in the technology market.*

Scaling and sustaining growth in a startup requires a strategic approach, balancing growth with sustainability. By understanding your growth limits and building strong, long-term partnerships, you can ensure your startup is well-positioned for continued success. Remember to assess your capacity, set realistic goals, and choose partners who align with your values and can scale with you. These strategies will help you navigate the complexities of growth and build a resilient, future-proof business.

# 16. Adapting to Market Changes

> In this chapter you will find:
>
> - Understanding Market Dynamics: Blue Oceans vs. Red Oceans
> - Continuous Learning: Staying Flexible and Adaptive

In the rapidly evolving business landscape, the ability to adapt to market changes is crucial for the sustained success of your startup. This chapter will delve into understanding market dynamics through the concepts of Blue Oceans and Red Oceans, and the importance of continuous learning to remain flexible and adaptive.

**Understanding Market Dynamics: Blue Oceans vs. Red Oceans**

One of the foundational concepts in understanding market dynamics is the distinction between Blue Oceans and Red Oceans, introduced by W. Chan Kim and Renée Mauborgne in their groundbreaking book "Blue Ocean Strategy." We try not to go into much detail in this book but this is something you should be aware of as it can help visualize things from a different perspective. Early in my career I attended a couple of different business schools. In one they told me executives have to fly above the ocean and understand how the different sharks behave. In the other, they told me executives have to learn how to swim between the sharks. I guess both have a similar meaning but where I want to go is you should understand this theory as it is widely used when you learn basic concepts of strategy development. So, here we go.

**Red Oceans**

Red Oceans represent all the industries in existence today – the known market space. In Red Oceans, industry boundaries are defined and accepted, and the competitive rules of the game are well understood. Companies try to outperform their rivals to grab a greater share of existing demand, leading to fierce competition. As the market space gets crowded, prospects for profits and growth diminish. Products become commodities, and the cutthroat nature of competition turns the ocean bloody, hence the term Red Oceans.

## Blue Oceans

In contrast, Blue Oceans denote all the industries not in existence today – the unknown market space, untainted by competition. In Blue Oceans, demand is created rather than fought over, and there is ample opportunity for growth that is both profitable and rapid. Blue Ocean Strategy involves finding or creating new market spaces that are free of competition. Instead of competing within the confines of existing industry norms, companies pursue differentiation and low cost simultaneously to open up a new market space and create new demand.

> ### Example: Cirque du Soleil
>
> *Cirque du Soleil is a prime example of a company that created a Blue Ocean. By blending elements of circus and theater, they created a unique entertainment experience that appealed to both traditional circus-goers and theater audiences. They redefined the circus industry, which was struggling in a Red Ocean of declining demand and high competition, and created a new market space with little to no competition.*

## Continuous Learning: Staying Flexible and Adaptive

Adapting to market changes requires a commitment to continuous learning and a willingness to stay flexible. Let's just list some strategies to help you remain adaptive in a dynamic market environment:

### 1. Monitor Market Trends and Consumer Behavior

Stay informed about the latest trends in your industry and shifts in consumer behavior. Regularly analyze market reports, attend industry conferences, and engage with customers to gain insights into emerging needs and preferences. Use this information to pivot your strategy and offerings as necessary.

## 2. Foster a Culture of Innovation

Encourage your team to think creatively and experiment with new ideas. Foster an environment where innovation is celebrated, and failures are viewed as learning opportunities. Implement regular brainstorming sessions, hackathons, and innovation workshops to keep the creative juices flowing.

## 3. Invest in Employee Development

Equip your team with the skills and knowledge they need to adapt to changing market conditions. Provide ongoing training and development opportunities, encourage cross-functional collaboration, and create a learning organization where knowledge sharing is the norm.

## 4. Agile and Lean Methodologies

Adopt agile and lean methodologies to increase your organization's responsiveness to change. These methodologies emphasize iterative development, customer feedback, and rapid prototyping, allowing you to quickly adapt to market changes and customer needs.

## 5. Scenario Planning

Engage in scenario planning to prepare for various potential future states of the market. By considering different scenarios, you can develop contingency plans and be better prepared to pivot your strategy when unexpected changes occur.

## 6. Customer Feedback Loops

Establish robust customer feedback loops to gather real-time insights into customer experiences and preferences. Use this feedback to continuously improve your products and services, ensuring they remain relevant and competitive. My recommendation is to have somebody appointed responsible for these loops! Usually, good senior product leads do an outstanding job and are able to link with sales and other units to make it happen.

> ### Example: Netflix
>
> *Netflix is a notable example of a company that has continuously adapted to market changes. Initially a DVD rental service, Netflix recognized the shift towards digital streaming and invested heavily in developing its streaming platform. Later, as competition in streaming intensified, they adapted again by producing original content, which has become a key differentiator. Their ability to stay flexible and respond to changing market dynamics has been a significant factor in their sustained success.*

**All in all..**

Adapting to market changes is essential for the long-term success of your startup. By understanding market dynamics through the lens of Blue Oceans and Red Oceans, and committing to continuous learning and flexibility, you can navigate the complexities of a dynamic business environment. Stay informed, foster innovation, invest in your team, and remain agile to ensure your startup not only survives but thrives amidst market changes.

# 17. SUSTAINABLE BUSINESS PRACTICES

> In this chapter you will find:
>
> - Building an Eco-Friendly Business
> - Corporate Social Responsibility
> - Long-Term Sustainability Strategies

I know, I know.. but we are no longer in 1950.. we have to talk about this, let's do it!

In today's world, building a business that prioritizes sustainability isn't just good for the planet—it's good for your bottom line. Customers, investors, and employees are increasingly looking to align with companies that demonstrate a genuine commitment to sustainable practices. In this chapter I will guide you through the key aspects of creating and maintaining a sustainable business, including building an eco-friendly business, embracing corporate social responsibility, and developing long-term sustainability strategies.

**Building an Eco-Friendly Business**

Creating an eco-friendly business starts with a commitment to minimizing your environmental footprint (it doesn't have to be expensive! For example, a digital first approach where documents are signed online whenever is possible!). Here are some actionable steps to get started:

**1. Assess Your Environmental Impact:** Begin by conducting an environmental audit to identify the areas where your business has the most significant impact. This includes everything from energy consumption and waste production to supply chain operations and product life cycles.

**2. Implement Energy-Efficient Practices:** Reduce your energy consumption by investing in energy-efficient appliances, lighting, and heating/cooling systems. Consider utilizing renewable energy sources such as solar or wind power. Encouraging remote work can also reduce your business's carbon footprint.

**3. Sustainable Sourcing:** Choose suppliers who prioritize sustainability. Look for certifications such as Fair Trade, organic, or those that demonstrate a commitment to environmental stewardship. By sourcing materials responsibly, you not only reduce your environmental impact but also support ethical practices globally.

**4. Waste Reduction:** Adopt practices that minimize waste production. This could involve implementing a recycling program, reducing packaging materials, or reusing and repurposing products. Encourage a culture of sustainability within your team by setting goals for waste reduction and celebrating achievements.

**5. Eco-Friendly Products:** Design products with sustainability in mind. This could mean using recycled or biodegradable materials, creating products that are durable and repairable, or offering recycling programs for your products.

**Corporate Social Responsibility**

Corporate Social Responsibility (CSR) is about going beyond profit to positively impact society. Here's how you can integrate CSR into your business model:

**1. Define Your CSR Goals:** Identify the social issues that align with your business values and where you can make the most significant impact. This could include supporting local communities, promoting education, or addressing social inequalities.

**2. Engage Employees:** Involve your employees in your CSR initiatives. Encourage volunteerism, provide opportunities for staff to participate in community projects, and match employee donations to charitable causes. Engaged employees are more likely to be motivated and committed to their work.

**3. Transparent Reporting:** Communicate your CSR efforts and achievements transparently. Publish regular reports that detail your initiatives, the progress you've made, and the impact you've had. Transparency builds trust with stakeholders and demonstrates your commitment to social responsibility. No, this is not about a single post a year on Linkedin on International Women's Day (after zero initiatives in the last twelve months) to say they support Women.. we are talking about something else, got it? ;)

**4. Partner with Non-Profits:** Collaborate with non-profit organizations that align with your CSR goals. Partnerships can amplify your impact and provide valuable resources and expertise to support your initiatives. And sometimes.. make it just for a better world. For example, you are in Digital Mental Health and your IT department has some laptops in good condition that will not be used in your company. Why not look for a local Non-Profit mental health center and give them for free?

**5. Ethical Business Practices:** Ensure that your business operations reflect your commitment to CSR. This includes fair labor practices, ethical sourcing, and promoting diversity and inclusion within your organization.

**Long-Term Sustainability Strategies**

Sustainability is a long-term commitment that requires strategic planning. Here are key strategies to ensure your business remains sustainable in the long run:

**1. Set Long-Term Goals:** Define clear, measurable sustainability goals that align with your business objectives. These goals should be ambitious yet achievable and should guide your decision-making process.

**2. Monitor and Measure Progress:** Regularly track and report on your sustainability initiatives. Use key performance indicators (KPIs) to measure your progress and make data-driven decisions to improve your practices continually. I know.. revenue KPIs first.. but also add something to reflect CSR and provide visibility.

**3. Innovate and Adapt:** Stay ahead of sustainability trends and innovations. Invest in research and development to find new ways to reduce your environmental impact and improve your sustainability practices. Being adaptable and open to change is crucial in the evolving landscape of sustainability.

**4. Educate and Train Employees:** Provide ongoing education and training for your employees on sustainability practices. Ensure that everyone in your organization understands the importance of sustainability and how they can contribute to achieving your goals.

**5. Stakeholder Engagement:** Engage with all your stakeholders, including customers, employees, investors, and the community, to gather feedback and collaborate on sustainability efforts. Building strong relationships and open communication channels will help you understand and meet the expectations of your stakeholders.

**6. Financial Planning:** Incorporate sustainability into your financial planning. Allocate resources for sustainability initiatives and consider the long-term financial benefits of sustainable practices, such as cost savings from energy efficiency and increased customer loyalty.

## All in all..

Sustainable business practices are no longer optional—they are essential for the long-term success and viability of your startup. By building an eco-friendly business, embracing corporate social responsibility, and implementing long-term sustainability strategies, you not only contribute positively to the environment and society but also create a resilient and future-proof business. Remember, sustainability is a journey, and every step you take brings you closer to a better future for your business and the world.

# 18. Innovation and Improvement

In this chapter you will find:

- Balancing Innovation with Improvement
- Reinventing the Wheel: When and How to Improve Existing Solutions

Innovation and continuous improvement are essential for the sustained growth and success of any startup. While innovation involves creating entirely new solutions, improvement focuses on enhancing existing processes, products, or services. Striking the right balance between the two can propel your startup to new heights. In this chapter, we will explore how to balance innovation with improvement and provide guidance on when and how to improve existing solutions effectively.

**Balancing Innovation with Improvement**

Balancing innovation with improvement is a delicate act that requires thoughtful consideration of your startup's goals, resources, and market conditions. Here are some proven strategies to achieve this balance:

**1. Align with Strategic Goals**

Ensure that both innovation and improvement efforts align with your startup's strategic goals. <u>Innovation should drive long-term growth and differentiation, while improvement should enhance operational efficiency and customer satisfaction</u>. Evaluate each initiative to determine its potential impact on your overall strategy (and.. as usual, prioritize if you do not have enough capacity to push them all).

## 2. Allocate Resources Wisely

Distribute resources between innovation and improvement based on your startup's current needs and market opportunities. Allocate sufficient budget, time, and talent to both areas, but remain flexible to shift resources as priorities change (and in startups.. they often change!). This dynamic allocation will help you stay agile and responsive to market demands.

## 3. Foster a Culture of Continuous Improvement

Cultivate a culture where continuous improvement is embedded in your team's mindset. Encourage employees to identify areas for enhancement and suggest solutions (One of the best startups I've been involved in, when an employee found a new potential improvement and implemented it then he received an economic compensation, that was a clear win-win situation!). Implement regular review processes to assess the effectiveness of improvements and make necessary adjustments.

## 4. Encourage Cross-Functional Collaboration

Promote collaboration between teams to leverage diverse perspectives and expertise. Cross-functional collaboration can lead to innovative ideas for improvement and help identify opportunities for innovation within existing processes. Break down silos and create an environment where knowledge sharing is encouraged. From my experience some startups struggle when opening new subsidiaries in foreign countries as some tend to operate independently, make sure there is alignment and the knowledge flows!

## 5. Measure and Evaluate

Establish metrics to measure the success of both innovation and improvement initiatives (# of new patents, USD saved, customer retention,...). Track key performance indicators (KPIs) to evaluate the impact on your startup's growth, efficiency, and customer satisfaction. Use data-driven insights to refine your approach and make informed decisions.

**Reinventing the Wheel: When and How to Improve Existing Solutions**

Improving existing solutions can be a more cost-effective and less risky approach compared to developing entirely new innovations. However, knowing when and how to improve existing solutions is crucial for maximizing benefits. Here are some guidelines to help you decide when to improve and how to do it effectively:

## 1. Identify Pain Points and Gaps

Regularly assess your products, services, and processes to identify pain points and gaps. Gather feedback from customers, employees, and stakeholders to pinpoint areas that need improvement. Look for recurring issues, inefficiencies, or unmet customer needs. There are very basic approaches to make it work.. For example, have you ever created a pareto diagram? Totally recommendable!

> *Example: Apple's Iterative Improvements*
>
> *Apple's approach to product development illustrates effective improvement of existing solutions. The company frequently releases updated versions of its products, such as the iPhone, incorporating incremental improvements based on user feedback and technological advancements. These iterative improvements enhance user experience and maintain customer loyalty.*

## 2. Prioritize High-Impact Areas

Focus on areas where improvements will have the most significant impact on your startup's performance and customer satisfaction. Prioritize enhancements that address critical issues, streamline operations, or deliver added value to customers. This prioritization ensures that your efforts yield meaningful results.

## 3. Leverage Technology and Innovation

Utilize technology and innovative techniques to enhance existing solutions. For example, implementing automation can streamline repetitive tasks, improving efficiency and reducing errors. (It may sound difficult but you can start with something very basic like digital signatures instead of handwritten when possible and then you move forward to more complex initiatives) Similarly, adopting advanced analytics can provide deeper insights into customer behavior, enabling you to refine your offerings.

**4. Implement a Phased Approach**

When improving existing solutions, consider implementing changes in phases. This phased approach allows you to test and validate improvements incrementally, reducing the risk of disruptions. Gather feedback at each stage and make necessary adjustments before rolling out changes on a larger scale.

> *Example: Amazon's Continuous Improvement*
>
> *Amazon's continuous improvement culture is evident in its logistics and fulfillment operations. The company consistently refines its processes to enhance delivery speed and efficiency. Innovations like the use of robotics in warehouses and optimization algorithms for delivery routes have significantly improved operational performance.*

**5. Communicate and Train**

Ensure that your team is informed and trained on any improvements made (new tools, sales playbook update, etc.). Clear communication and training help employees understand the benefits of the changes and how to implement them effectively. This support fosters a smooth transition and maximizes the impact of improvements.

# All in all..

Balancing innovation with improvement is essential for the sustained success of your startup. By aligning initiatives with strategic goals, allocating resources wisely, fostering a culture of continuous improvement, encouraging cross-functional collaboration, and measuring outcomes, you can effectively balance both aspects. Additionally, knowing when and how to improve existing solutions by identifying pain points, prioritizing high-impact areas, leveraging technology, implementing phased changes, and ensuring effective communication will help you enhance your startup's performance and stay competitive in a dynamic market. Embrace the dual approach of innovation and improvement to drive growth and create lasting value for your customers and stakeholders.

# ONE LAST THING...

I hope you enjoyed this book and found it useful on your entrepreneurial journey. Your support truly makes a difference. If you could take a moment to post a short review on Amazon, I would be incredibly grateful. Your feedback not only helps other readers discover this book but also guides us in improving future editions. Thank you for being a part of this journey.

Other titles available from myself:

# FROM PROJECT MANAGER TO PROGRAM MANAGER

## STRATEGIES FOR ELEVATING YOUR CAREER

WRITTEN BY
**MARION PARKER**

www.ingramcontent.com/pod-product-compliance
Lightning Source LLC
Chambersburg PA
CBHW071949210526
45479CB00003B/869